Contents

Living Down the Family Name   2

The Marble Man   4

First Assignment   5

Lee and the Mexican-American War   6

John Brown's Raid   8

Fort Sumter and the Outbreak of the Civil War   10

"King of Spades"   12

Lee Takes Command of the Army of Northern Virginia   14

Lee Invades the North   16

The Battle of Antietam   17

The Battle of Fredricksburg   19

Chancellorsville: Lee's Most Masterful Battle   21

Gettysburg: The High Water Mark of the Confederacy   23

Grant Comes East   26

Siege of Petersburg   28

Lee Surrenders at Appomattox Court House   30

The Post-War Years   32

Living Down the Family Name

ROBERT E. LEE was born on January 19, 1807, in the Lee family mansion (Stratford Hall) in Virginia's Westmoreland County. He was the fifth of six children born to Harry "Light Horse Harry" Lee and his second wife Ann Hill (Carter) Lee. Named after Ann's two favorite brothers, the boy came into the world at a time when his mother's health, and his father's finances, were both failing.

Robert's father, Light Horse Harry, earned his nickname as a dashing cavalry commander during the Revolutionary War. he had been one of George Washington's favorite officers but resigned his commission in 1782 while the war was still under way. Harry Lee and George Washington remained close. As president, Washington helped Lee attain political office and selected him to lead Federal troops in putting down the so-called "Whiskey Rebellion" in 1794. Five years later, Harry Lee was elected to Congress and, upon Washington's death in 1801, delivered the famous eulogy "first in war, first in peace, first in the hearts of his countrymen."

Ann Hill Carter, Robert's mother, came from a distinguished Virginia family. As the daughter of Charles Carter, a wealthy plantation owner, she grew up accustomed to the finer things in life. Ann was twenty years old when she and Harry Lee, then governor of Virginia and seventeen years her senior, were married. The ceremony was held at the ancestral Carter residence at Shirley, a plantation located along the north bank of the James River some twenty miles southeast of Richmond. Literally, it was union of fame and fortune.

Despite having all the advantages that money and power might bring to a newlywed couple, the marriage was an unhappy one. Harry Lee was an inveterate land speculator and spendthrift. Having gone through his first wife's fortune, he seemed determined to do the same again. Over a ten year period the size of the Lee family estate was reduced from sixty-five hundred acres to less than two thousand as Harry sold off portions in a losing effort to stay ahead of his creditors. In 1809, when Robert was just two years old, Harry's creditor's finally caught up with him and sent him to prison.

The following year, shortly after Harry was released, the family moved to Alexandria. What was left of Stratford became the property of Henry Lee IV, son of Harry's first wife. Life in Alexandria brought young Robert into close contact with members of his extended family. Though he mixed well, he was by all accounts shy and somewhat reserved. By the time Robert turned six years old, his father had left the country, seeking to repair his fortune throughout the Caribbean. Harry's sole written mention of the son he hardly knew was that "Robert was always good, and will be confirmed in his happy turn of mind by his ever watchful and affectionate mother."

Stratford Hall, Lee's birthplace and home of the Lee family. The surrounding plantation was gradually sold off to help pay off debts owed by the insolvent Harry Lee. The house passed from the Lee family in 1822 when it was sold by Henry Lee (IV), Harry Lee's son by his first marriage.

Light Horse Harry Lee died in 1818 without ever again seeing the family he had abandoned. Though Robert did not outwardly despair of his father's absence, he would spend some time later in life re-editing Harry Lee's memoirs in an effort to cast him in a more favorable light. Robert heard of his father's death at age eleven, but it wasn't until 1862, when he presumably had more important things on his mind, that he first visited his father's grave in Dungeness, Georgia. In 1870, the last year of his life, Robert made a second, and final pilgrimage to Dungeness, perhaps still hoping to come to terms with his father's memory.

The home of William Fitzhugh, a distant relative, at 607 Oronoco Street (near center) in Alexandria where Lee lived with his mother and five siblings.

With Harry Lee out of the picture, responsibility for raising six children fell to Ann. In this, she seems to have managed quite well despite her often poor health and limited budget. Conscious of her husband's poor example, Ann spent much of her time instilling within her children a sense of positive virtues. For Robert, this meant learning his catechism and attending church regularly. While Ann was evangelical and looked at religion as a means of forging a personal relationship with Jesus, Robert saw sin in terms of self control. If Robert appeared shy and reserved, it was an exercise in piety, of selflessness, and a sincere desire to avoid conflict of any kind. Above all things, this was his mother's legacy.

The Marble Man

As LEE ENTERED adulthood, he naturally began to consider his future. Given his father's example, a career in the military was probably not his first choice, but it was within the family's means. If accepted at the United States Military Academy at West Point, the cost of his education would be born by the taxpayers. Besides, as the son of an important officer like Light Horse Harry Lee, young Robert would be able to continue the family tradition. Shortly after Robert's seventeenth birthday, he met to discuss his admission with Secretary of War John C. Calhoun, acting 'gatekeeper' to the Point. The meeting went well, and in 1825 Robert joined the ranks as a cadet.

Robert E. Lee as depicted in a painting by William E. West, 1838.

Lee adapted quickly to the spartan existence of a West Point plebe, quite comfortable in an environment where self control and discipline were coin of the realm. He did well in all his courses but excelled in engineering, the *ne plus ultra* of a West Point education. When the class standing for 1829 was published, Lee finished second. The only man to finish ahead of him was Charles Mason; who, after serving out his military obligation in ordinary fashion, resigned his commission and returned to civilian life.

It should be noted that Lee managed to graduate from West Point without a single demerit charged to his name. (A demerit is an administrative black mark on a cadet's record earned as a result of some infraction of the rules and assessed according to the severity of the transgression.) In Lee's day, demerits could be removed by performing extra duty such as standing watch so it is unclear how many (if any) were actually levied against him. In any case, graduating without demerits in those days was not uncommon. Four other cadets in the class of 1829 matched Lee's spotless record.

4

With his time at West Point behind him, Lee could reflect upon the monastic life he had entered as a boy of seventeen. The academy changed him, defined him, and gave him a creative outlet for his talents. He emerged a man, flush with joy in his own success and accomplishment. Gone now was the aloof shyness. In its place was a confident military bearing, an unpretentious dignified poise that he wore without a hint of stiffness. Many of Lee's classmates noticed the transformation and commented upon how his handsome features appeared etched from stone. Among his closest friends, the statuesque Lee became known as the 'Marble Model'.

First Assignments

UPON HIS GRADUATION, Lee earned a commission as a 2nd Lieutenant of Engineers and returned home once again. It was an unhappy homecoming. Lee's mother, Ann, died less than a month after he arrived. The tuberculosis that had been steadily sapping her strength for years finally ended her life in July 1829. With the death of his mother, Lee was now an orphan at age twenty-two. The stay at home was mercifully short given the circumstances. In August, the Army Corps of Engineers sent word that Lee was to report for his first duty assignment to Cockspur Island in the Savannah River. At Cockspur, he would assist in the construction of a fort intended to protect the city of Savannah from naval attack. The fort eventually became known as Fort Pulaski and would figure prominently during the Civil War to come.

In 1831, Lee was reassigned to Fort Monroe, a post located at the tip of the James River peninsula. The new proximity to family and friends gave Lee the opportunity to resume his courtship of Mary Ann Randolph Custis, daughter and only child of George Washington Parke Custis, grandson of Mary Washington (wife of George Washington) by a previous marriage. Mary Custis grew up at Mount Vernon, basking in all the attention afforded her station in life. She had a stable home, money, slaves and the prestige of a good family name. In short, Mary had everything that Lee's mother Ann had wanted during her life. Perhaps there was a bit of Ann Lee inside of Robert pushing him into taking Mary as a wife. On June 30, 1831, Robert and Mary were married at her Arlington home. The first of their seven children, George Washington Custis Lee was born on September 16, 1832.

Lee and the Mexican-American War

American troops enter Mexico City in September 1847. Many familiar Civil War leaders, both blue and gray, participated in the campaign.

On MARCH 1, 1845, the Republic of Texas was formally annexed by the United States despite saber-rattling from Mexico that such an act would mean war. Many in government probably hoped for war as an opportunity to continue the country's "manifest destiny." It took just over a year but on May 13, 1846, the United States declared war on Mexico. Suddenly hundreds of West Point graduates found their services very much in demand, including one bored officer of engineers named Robert E. Lee.

In August 1846, Lee received orders assigning him to Major General John E. Wool's army gathering in San Antonio. Anxious for adventure (and possibly a chance at promotion), Captain Lee enthusiastically accompanied the army into northern Mexico. Wool's men marched more than seven hundred miles, but on the whole saw little combat. Lee was subsequently transferred from this backwater campaign and assigned to what ultimately became the main event (General Winfield Scott's landing at Vera Cruz and march on Mexico City.

Lee went to Mexico City with Scott as a member of his engineering staff. In 1847, he scouted out a route by which Scott's army outflanked Santa Anna at Cerro Gordo. The battle was a decisive victory for the Americans and because of his actions Lee was promoted some months later to brevet (temporary) Major. It was the first of three such promotions he would receive. During his time in Mexico, Lee built bridges, made survey maps, conducted reconnaissance, and directed artillery fire like a veteran artillerist. By the time the battles around Mexico City were over, Lee was a brevet Colonel. On June 29, 1948, Lee returned home to Arlington a war hero.

Victory in the Mexican-American War did much to shape the conduct of the American Civil War. It brought together the entire officer corps, both North and South, in a shared experience. Friendships begun in the barracks at West Point were strengthened on the playing fields of Buena Vista and Molino del Rey. One day these same men would be busy killing each other, but in the meantime, service in Mexico provided them with a common enemy. It was a training ground, a place where future blue and gray generals learned their trade as Captains and Lieutenants. Much of the insight Lee would later display during the Civil War was undoubtedly related to his time in Mexico. It was also where Lee learned that wars are won by taking ground, not defending it.

Colonel Robert E. Lee (1850-1852). Note the prominent chin and dark mustache. All who observed Lee throughout his life commented upon his good looks.

Immediately after the war, Colonel Lee was sent to Baltimore to assist in the construction of Fort Carroll off Soller's Point. It was a job very much like his first assignment in Savannah. The task completed, Lee next received orders to report to West Point and assume the position of Superintendent. From 1852 to 1855, Lee discharged the duties of Superintendent though he was uncomfortable being the center of attention in an academic world. The assignment kept him in close contact with his mentor, Winfield Scott, and gave him the opportunity to know the men who would one day make up the nation's officer corps.

In 1855, Lee transferred from the Engineer Corps to the Cavalry Corps. Soon after, he was placed in charge of the 2nd US Cavalry Regiment stationed in Camp Cooper, Texas. It was the first field command of his career. Except for a brief foray against a small group of Comanches, most of Lee's time was spent presiding over courts-martial. While Lee was away, Mary's father died leaving her with an estate consisting of more than five thousand acres and one hundred fifty slaves. The death of his father-in-law gave Lee an excuse to return to Arlington in 1857, whereupon he became the de facto executor of his father-in-law's troublesome will.

Robert E. Lee as depicted in a commissioned painting by Robert W. Weir (cir. 1853). Lee at this time was Superintendent of the Military Academy at West Point.

Far from being a windfall, George Washington Parke Custis left his daughter a run-down estate and more debt than Light Horse Harry could ever have imagined. After being granted an extended leave of absence from the army, Lee approached his new responsibilities with characteristic determination. Being thrust into the position of a classic slave-holding plantation owner made him uneasy. Though very much a man of his time with regard to the separation of the races, Lee considered the institution of slavery "a moral and political evil." While it might be evil, he still considered it necessary for maintaining the existing racial hierarchy.

John Brown's Raid

In OCTOBER 1859, while Lee was still on leave in Arlington, a militant abolitionist by the name of John Brown took over the Federal arsenal in Harper's Ferry, Virginia. Often called the catalyst of the Civil War, John Brown's raid on Harper's Ferry was only the first step in his dream of igniting an armed slave revolt throughout the South. His action awakened fears not felt in Virginia since Nat Turner's Rebellion of 1831. The great slave uprising he hoped to create never materialized, however. Found guilty of treason some weeks later, John Brown was sentenced to death by hanging and executed on December 2, 1859.

In Lee's mind, the whole affair was of little consequence. After reporting to the War Department in Washington, Lee was dispatched to Harper's Ferry along with eighty U.S. Marines from the Washington Naval Yard. Upon his arrival, Lee discovered that some local militia units from nearby Charles Town had John Brown and his followers contained inside the Armory Engine House. Lee's Marines simply charged the Engine House and after a brief struggle, John Brown and his men were taken into custody.

At Harper's Ferry in 1859, Colonel Lee and a detachment of U.S. Marines storm the Federal Arsenal's engine house held by John Brown's raiders.

As the drum beat to war grew louder and faster throughout the winter of 1860-61, Lee was writing long letters to family and friends hinting at what his course of action might be if war broke out. One such correspondence contained his oft-repeated position, "I prize the Union very highly & know of no personal sacrifice that I would not make to preserve it, save that of honor." In a letter to his wife in January, Lee wrote, "As far as I can judge from the papers, we [the country] are between a state of anarchy & civil war." On the same day, Lee sent these words to his son Custis "The South, in my opinion, has been aggrieved by the acts of the North. I feel the aggression and am willing to take every proper step for redress." Later in the same letter he wrote, "If the Union is dissolved and the Government disrupted, I shall return to my native state and share the miseries of my people, and save in defense will draw my sword on none."

> *"I am one of those dull creatures that cannot see the good of secession."*
> — Robert E. Lee, 1861

By February 1861, a total of seven Southern states had seceded from the United States to form a new nation; the Confederate States of America. The following month, Lee was ordered to turn over his command of the 2nd Cavalry Regiment in Texas and return once again to Washington. By the time he arrived in Washington, Abraham Lincoln had already taken the oath of office and announced that the Federal government would fight, if necessary, to retain its possessions. One Federal possession that Lincoln intended on retaining was Fort Sumter, a masonry fort located just inside the entrance to Charleston harbor.

Fort Sumter and the Outbreak of Civil War

The Arlington home of Robert E. Lee shown here after being occupied by Union troops in 1861.

SOUTH CAROLINIANS looked upon Fort Sumter as an affront to their state sovereignty. Demands that Lincoln surrender the fort were ignored and when Federal ships attempted to resupply the garrison, on April 12, 1861, Confederate guns surrounding the fort opened fire. Less than a week later, Virginia legislators voted to secede from the Union, a measure that would be confirmed by popular referendum on May 23rd. On the very day Virginia was opting to join her sister states in rebellion, Lee was in Washington visiting Winfield Scott one last time. Lee was offered the top spot in Lincoln's army if he would lead it against the Confederacy. Lee refused, unable to contemplate going to war against his native state. Scott, himself, a Virginian, probably understood Lee's reluctance and was sorry to see him resign.

Lee remained a civilian for exactly five days. On April 22, Governor John Letcher offered him command of Virginia's land and naval forces at the rank of Major General. The offer was quickly accepted. In May, the capital of the Confederacy was moved from Montgomery, Alabama to Richmond. From a political standpoint, the move made sense. Virginia was the most populous of all Southern states and had a majority of the South's heavy industry concentrated within its borders. From a military standpoint however, the decision virtually guaranteed undue attention would be placed upon Richmond and that the city, so close to Washington, would become an inviting target.

Shortly after Jefferson Davis and his government entourage arrived in Richmond, Virginia's state militia was nationalized. Lee's main task became integrating Virginia's forces into the Confederate army. This accomplished, he was essentially out of a job. Though he and Jefferson Davis were close and had worked together in the past, Lee's future role in the war was by no means certain. He sat out the first major battle of the war though it took place less than one hundred miles away. The battle of Manassas, or Bull Run as it was known in the North, was a stunning Confederate victory.

Using the dates of their commissions as a means of determining seniority, on August 31, the Confederate Congress confirmed its top five general officers. The highest-ranking officer of the five was Samuel Cooper. As Adjutant and Inspector General, his position remained that of an administrative aid to Jefferson Davis throughout the war. Second in command was Albert Sidney Johnston, a very capable field officer who commanded Southern troops in the West until his death at the battle of Shiloh in 1862. Next came Robert E. Lee. His promotion to Brigadier General was backdated by the Congress to May 14, 1861. Fourth was Joseph E. Johnston, who along with the fifth officer on the list, Pierre Gustave Toutant Beauregard, were responsible for the Confederate victory at Manassas.

"King of Spades"

DESPITE HIS SENIORITY, Lee was something of a fifth wheel during those early months of the war. Though Davis deferred to Lee's judgment on military matters, there were too many officers and too few troops to go around. Lee would simply have to wait to obtain a field command of his own. In July, as the Union offensive in northwestern Virginia gathered steam, Davis sent Lee there to act as an overseer and presidential advisor. Confederate officers on the scene resented his sudden presence. Without command authority, he was unable to elicit their cooperation or even get them to stop squabbling amongst each other. Union troops took advantage of the situation and drove Confederate forces from the region.

Lee soon found out that newspaper editors do not like defeated generals. Many in the South took to calling him "Granny Lee", for the way he had avoided combat in favor of maneuver in northwestern Virginia. The fact that he was not in direct command of combat troops didn't seem to matter much to those searching for a scapegoat. As the senior ranking officer on the scene, Lee must have been responsible. Fortunately, Davis was not a man to give in to public pressure and declined to sack Lee for the sake of political expediency. Instead, Lee was handed a much greater challenge, and one more suited to his background as an engineer.

Convinced that a Union naval flotilla was about to attack Port Royal, South Carolina, Secretary of War, Judah P. Benjamin put Lee in charge of the coastal defenses of eastern Florida, Georgia, and South Carolina. Given the length of the coastline and the lack of adequate men and guns, Lee

George Washington Custis Lee, eldest son of Robert E. Lee, attended West Point and graduated first in the class of 1854. He served on the president's staff as an officer of engineers until late in the war and attained the rank of Major General in 1864.

Robert E. Lee (center) with Generals Beauregard, Johnston, and Longstreet.

immediately concluded that an attempt to defend everything would spread his forces and in the end, they would defend nothing. He proposed withdrawing from the coastal regions, out of range of Union warships, and concentrating his meager resources only at those areas deemed vital. The lesson of Port Royal, which fell before he arrived, was that the Federal navy had the power to conduct operations just about anywhere it chose. Nothing in range of its guns would be safe for long.

The strategy of withdrawing from the coast in favor of fighting a mobile battle in-land was a prudent one, but it didn't sit well with plantation owners whose land would be sacrificed to a Union advance. Rice and cotton growers throughout the coastal region protested. Calling him "Evacuating Lee" or "King of Spades" after his penchant for digging fortifications, they fought his plan all the way to Richmond. Davis was again forced to weather the political fallout on behalf of Lee, a general who might have had seniority but had not yet won a battle. In March 1862, he recalled Lee to Richmond to serve as his military advisor.

Lee Takes Command of the Army of Northern Virginia

BY THE TIME Lee arrived in the capitol chances for a Confederate victory never looked more bleak. A massive Union army under General George B. McClellan lay north of the James River, seemingly ready to swallow up Richmond at a moment's notice. Two more Union armies sat astride the Shenandoah threatening to drive Southern troops from this vital breadbasket. When Davis asked Lee where the next line of defense should be constructed if Richmond fell, Lee snapped back, "Richmond must not fall, it must not be given up." Happy with the answer, Davis put Lee in charge of the army after General Johnston fell seriously wounded at the battle of Seven Pines (known in the North as Fair Oaks).

On June 1, 1862, as the battle of Seven Pines was wearing down, Lee formally took command of the army. One of his first official acts was to designate his command the Army of Northern Virginia. More than just a simple name change, it was a statement of intent. This army was not going to retreat from Virginia and Richmond was not going to be given up. When McClellan heard that Lee had assumed command, he remarked, "I prefer Lee to Johnston. The former [Lee] is too cautious and weak under grave responsibility. Personally brave and energetic to a fault, he yet is wanting in moral firmness when pressed by heavy responsibility, and is likely to be timid and irresolute in action." Lee would soon give McClellan ample cause to take back these words.

Taking the lessons learned in Mexico to heart, Lee was determined to drive the Union army away from Richmond rather than wait to be attacked. On June 12, Lee directed James Ewell Brown (J.E.B.) Stuart, his able cavalry commander, to scout out the Union army and discover its weak spots. After riding completely around the Union army, Stuart returned with the news that McClellan's right flank was "in the air," meaning that it was not anchored by terrain and therefore vulnerable to attack. This piece of information touched off a series of running battles known collectively as the Seven Days campaign.

From June 25, to July 1, Lee's Army of Northern Virginia delivered a number of hammer-blows to McClellan's flanks hoping to cut off his army from its base of supply. Believing himself outnumbered, for why else would the Confederates be attacking, McClellan withdrew to the James River. There the big guns of the Federal Navy were in position to provide his army with some measure of protection. It was a stunning reversal of fortune. McClellan had been so close to Richmond his men could hear its church bells being rung. One week later, the Army of the Potomac lay cowering at Harrison Landing, lucky to have escaped the battle of annihilation Lee had intended.

> *"Yes, he will get away because I cannot have my orders carried out."*
> —Robert E. Lee replying to a staff member's observation that McClellan was escaping

In time, the Army of Northern Virginia would become a personal extension of Lee in much the same way as the Army of the Potomac became McClellan's. But unlike McClellan and his massive Union host, Lee and his army drew close as partners in adversity are apt to do. Their attacks during the Seven Days battles were driven home with a ferocity that shook McClellan. Unfortunately for Lee, not enough time had passed for the army to function as smoothly as it should. Orders were misunderstood or ignored and subordinates often failed to exercise initiative. Lee missed a golden opportunity to destroy the Army of the Potomac, but not for lack of trying.

The Seven Days battles were a demonstration of the differences between the two commanders. In commenting on Lee, McClellan was amazingly off the mark. Lee, on the other hand, showed himself to be a good judge of character. This ability to "read" his opponent was a secret of his success. He could often define the enemy's intentions and use this knowledge to great advantage. In McClellan's case, Lee played on his worst fear (the safety of his army) and was able to seize the initiative. So effective was Lee's counterattack that McClellan was completely unnerved by the time he reached the James River.

General Thomas J. Jackson, better known as "Stonewall" Jackson. Though Jackson failed Lee miserably during the Seven Days Battles, he is generally regarded as one of Lee's better staff officers.

> *"The shot that struck me down is perhaps the very best that has been fired for our Southern cause yet. For I possess in no degree the confidence of our government, and now they have in my place one who does..."*
> — Joseph E. Johnston commenting on his replacement)

15

Lee Invades the North

WITH MCCLELLAN'S Peninsula campaign all but over, a new Union army under the command of Major General John Pope started moving toward Richmond from the north. Of all the Union commanders Lee would face during the war, none provoked his ire as much as John Pope. Pope was given to bluster and braggadocio. He trumpeted his recent victories at New Madrid and Island No. 10 in such a way as to belittle his new soldiers. "I come to you from the West", he said, "where we have always seen the backs of our enemies." The army, he declared, would live off the land, execute anyone found engaging in sabotage or guerrilla warfare, and would require all citizens to take an oath of loyalty or see their belongings confiscated. In essence, Pope was declaring war upon the people of Virginia, something that McClellan had conspicuously avoided.

To Lee, a native Virginian, Pope was a "miscreant", a criminal, not a military commander. As soon as he was convinced that McClellan's army was being withdrawn from the James River, Lee gave Jackson a portion of his army and sent him north with orders that Pope be "suppressed". Far from being suppressed, Pope got the better of Jackson at Cedar Mountain on August 9th. Instead of following up however, Pope halted his army near Culpepper for a time then withdrew back across the Rappahannock River to await the arrival of McClellan's forces. Having missed his chance to destroy McClellan on the peninsula, Lee was determined to smash Pope before the two could affect a link-up.

Hoping to turn the Union right flank, Lee sent Jackson on an end run around the Bull Run Mountains. The maneuver put Jackson's entire force, twenty-three thousand men in all, squarely astride Pope's line of supply. After spending a day burning the Union depot at Manassas, Jackson deployed his men along an unfinished railroad cut just west of the old 1861 battlefield. Believing Jackson to be retreating, Pope gave orders to pursue. On August 29th, Pope launched several unsuccessful attacks. The following day, as Pope renewed his attack on Jackson, the other wing of Lee's army arrived unnoticed. This wing, led by Major General James Longstreet, caught Pope's army by surprise and threw it back across the Bull Run River. The second battle of Manassas, like the first, was a stunning Confederate victory.

The Battle of Antietam

In SEPTEMBER 1862, Lee and the Army of Northern Virginia crossed the Potomac River into Maryland. Although he hoped to spark a general uprising and rally many Marylanders to his flag, Lee's immediate objective was to reach the Susquehanna River in southern Pennsylvania and destroy the bridges there. Coupled with the capture of Harper's Ferry, loss of the Susquehanna bridges would sever Washington D.C. from the Ohio River. Ultimately, Lee intended to capture Philadelphia, Baltimore, or both as circumstances permitted. Of course, he expected the Union army to try and stop him, in fact, he counted on it. It would give him an opportunity to fight his one big war-winning battle of annihilation.

Pope's tenure as commander of the Army of the Potomac was mercifully brief after his drubbing at Second Manassas. Though he was loath to do so, Lincoln put McClellan back in command. Whatever faults he might possess, McClellan was an able administrator and this was what Lincoln needed most. Soon after his reinstatement, McClellan got one of the biggest breaks of the war. A copy of Lee's entire battle plan (Special Orders #191), complete with troop locations, unit strengths, and campaign intentions, was discovered by Union pickets outside Frederick, Md. McClellan now held a blueprint for destroying Lee.

Fitzhugh Lee, nephew of Robert E. Lee, graduated from West Point in 1856, forty-fifth out of a class of forty-nine. During the war, Lee served with distinction as a cavalry officer under J.E.B Stuart and attained the rank of Major General in 1863.

17

Robert E. Lee depicted in a photograph taken in 1862. The dark mustache and clean shaven face have disappeared in favor of a full gray beard.

McClellan seemed to grasp his good fortune and exclaimed, "Here is a paper with which if I cannot beat Bobby Lee, I will be willing to go home." The captured documents clearly showed that the Confederate army was not nearly as strong as he thought. More importantly, McClellan could see that it was strung out from Pennsylvania to Virginia. If he moved quickly enough, he could destroy Lee before he had a chance to regroup. But in a situation that called for the utmost speed, McClellan characteristically allowed almost a full day to pass before issuing his orders. It was all the time Lee needed to concentrate his army and prepare for McClellan's attack.

On September 17, 1862, McClellan attacked Lee along the meandering Antietam Creek just north of Sharpsburg, Md. The battle of Antietam (known as Sharpsburg in the South) was the war's bloodiest single day. By nightfall, more than twenty-five thousand men, both blue and gray, lay dead or wounded. Because of McClellan's hesitant advance, Lee had just enough time to mass his far-flung army. Counting out stragglers, he was lucky to have just under forty-five thousand men ready for battle, only half as many as McClellan had at his disposal. Rather than use his numerical advantage to simply steam-roll the worn out Confederates, McClellan launched three poorly coordinated attacks that were each turned back with heavy casualties.

A bitter harvest; Confederate dead along the edge of Miller's Cornfield at the battle of Antietam, September 17, 1862.

At Sharpsburg, Lee averted what could have been a disaster but the battle put an end to his hopes of reaching the Susquehanna, Philadelphia, or anywhere else. Nearly a third of his army, some fourteen thousand men, were lost. After the battle, he made the most of McClellan's cautious nature and withdrew back across the Potomac. Although the victory at Antietam provided Lincoln with a venue for his Emancipation Proclamation, he was furious at the failure to destroy Lee's army. McClellan was sacked shortly thereafter and replaced by Major General Ambrose Burnside. Upon hearing the news of McClellan's dismissal, Lee observed, "I fear they will continue to make changes till they find someone I don't understand."

The Battle of Fredricksburg

Lee and Longstreet view the slaughter from atop Marye's Heights. The battle of Fredricksburg came close to wrecking the Army of the Potomac.

FOLLOWING THE REPULSE of his northern invasion, Lee retired to Virginia to rebuild what was left of his army. Rebuilding was no doubt going to be difficult since Antietam had claimed the lives of many experienced soldiers. His ten divisions were down to less than thirty-five thousand men. To fill the ranks, Lee would be forced to use an increasing number of young men, old men, and those caught up in the nation's first draft. As much as Lee might prize offensive action, his losses at Sharpsburg handed the initiative back to the North. The ball, so to speak, was in Mr. Lincoln's court.

To get the ball rolling, Lincoln prodded Burnside, his new commanding general, into moving south at the head of an army some one hundred and thirty thousand strong. Burnside's plan was to shift his attack so that the army could be supplied more easily by sea. He had hoped to get across the Rappahannock at Fredricksburg before Lee could react, but the pontoon bridges he had requested failed to arrive. By the time Burnside crossed the river, Lee had seventy-five thousand men entrenched atop Mayre's Heights, blocking his path. The battle thus joined, Burnside did exactly as Lee had hoped; in fact, Union troops could hardly have been moved to suit Lee better than if he had positioned them himself.

"It is well that war is so terrible, or we should grow too fond of it"

— Robert E. Lee at the battle of Fredricksburg

Major General Ambrose Burnside showing a style of facial hair that would one day come to be known by a derivative of his name. Burnside was relieved after presiding over the deaths of thousands at Fredricksburg.

On December 13, 1862, a massive phalanx of Union troops started up the slopes toward Lee's waiting army. It was open ground, every foot of which was covered by a hundred Confederate muskets looking down from above. An aid to Longstreet said, "General, a chicken could not live on that field when we open up on it." Burnside's attack was met with a hail of shot and shell that tore apart its neat battle lines. The men re-formed and charged again, and yet again. Union troops made fourteen charges up Marye's Heights, one right after another. By the end of the day, more than twelve thousand of Burnside's men lay dead or wounded. Lee lost less than half this number. Surviving members of the Army of the Potomac pulled back across the Rappahannock River two days later. Burnside, who had once protested his promotion to Lincoln, professing incompetence, was relieved shortly thereafter.

Chancellorsville: Lee's Most Masterful Battle

Lee at Chancellorsville. His victory over Hooker was a masterstroke though it cost him the life of Stonewall Jackson and set in motion events leading up to Gettysburg.

AFTER FREDERICKSBURG, the two sides maneuvered briefly then went into winter quarters on opposite banks of the Rappahannock. In January, command of the Union army went to Major General Joseph "Fighting Joe" Hooker, a profane, hard drinking West Pointer who talked too much for his own good. In the spring, Lincoln wrote to him, "Go forward, and bring us victories." Hooker replied, "My plans are perfect, and when I start to carry them out, may God have mercy on Bobby Lee; for I shall have none."

Hooker was likely unaware but at this very point in time, God was indeed showing his mercy to Booby Lee. In late March, Lee became seriously ill. He complained in a letter to his wife of doctors "tapping him like an old steam boiler". For the better part of a month, Lee remained bed-ridden and was, in his own words, "feeble & worthless". The nature of the illness defied precise diagnosis at the time, but the symptoms, if described today, sound suspiciously like arteriosclerosis. Lee made steady improvement throughout April and May, but he never completely recovered. Cardiovascular problems would continue to plague him for the rest of his life.

Back in February, Lee displayed his canny insight into the new Union commander. "General Hooker is obliged to do something. I do not know what it will be. He is playing the Chinese game; trying what frightening will do. He runs out his guns, starts his wagons and

"He has lost his left arm, but I have lost my right."

—Robert E. Lee upon hearing of Jackson's misfortune at Chancellorsville

A famous photograph of Robert E. Lee atop Traveller, a horse he purchased for $200. Traveller remained with Lee throughout the war

troops up & down the river and creates an excitement generally. Our men look in wonder, give a cheer & all again subsides...". On April 29, the Chinese game Hooker was playing ended. He, along with five Union corps, crossed the Rappahannock above Fredricksburg while another two corps (under General John Sedgewick) crossed below. Hooker's plan was obvious; he intended to trap Lee inside a gigantic pincer movement.

Though already outnumbered two to one, Lee left Jackson at Fredricksburg to handle Sedgewick while he and the bulk of the army moved to confront Hooker in a heavily wooded region known as the "Wilderness". Inexplicably, Hooker halted his flanking maneuver as soon as he made contact with Lee near Chancellorsville. He was unsure of Lee's exact whereabouts because his cavalry had been sent off to threaten Lee's supply line. Lee, on the other hand, had Stuart's cavalry close at hand and knew of Hooker's vulnerable right flank. Having divided his army once, Lee proposed to divide it yet again.

On May 2, while he faced down Hooker at Chancellorsville, Lee sent Jackson's corps on another end run around the Union army. It was the decisive moment of the battle. Jackson struck from the rear while Lee continued to demonstrate in front. Hooker, who had intended to trap Lee, was himself caught in a trap and crushed. Lee's jubilance over this latest victory was tempered by the news that "Stonewall" Jackson was severely wounded and forced to lose a limb. Within a week, Jackson would be dead from pneumonia.

Early in the war, there were those who confessed their doubts about Lee, calling him "Granny Lee" or "King of Spades". After Chancellorsville, all doubts were gone. Far from being "timid and irresolute", Lee was in the words of one of his staff officers "audacity personified." Chancellorsville was perhaps his greatest battle. Despite being outnumbered, he showed what an army could do under effective leadership. Hooker, on the other hand, talked a good game but choked under pressure. Later, when asked about the reason for his defeat, Hooker said, "To tell you the truth, I just lost confidence in Joe Hooker." Self doubt was a problem that Lee never had to contend with.

Gettysburg: The High Water Mark of the Confederacy

IT HAS BEEN SAID that Gettysburg was the price the South paid for having Robert E. Lee. Others have called it the Confederacy's high-water mark. It was the place where the Southern tide swept in, crested, then receded with astonishing rapidity. No matter what analogy you wish to use; Gettysburg was the largest battle ever fought in this hemisphere and it was the bloodiest single battle of the American Civil War. Over the course of three days, more than fifty thousand men were killed, wounded, or simply missing.

Lee's army crossing the Potomac River. The Potomac served as the de facto dividing line between the two sides throughout the war.

Following his victory at Chancellorsville, a decision was made for another invasion of the North. Before Lee started out however, the Army of Northern Virginia went through an organizational overhaul. Instead of the "wing" concept, Lee broke his army up into three corps of three divisions each. By reducing the size of his corps, he hoped to improve upon their responsiveness and make them less difficult to control. With Jackson dead, Lee's three corps commanders were James Longstreet (I corps), Richard Ewell (II Corps) and Ambrose P. Hill (III corps). J.E.B. Stuart remained in charge of Lee's cavalry consisting of five brigades plus horse artillery. All together, in the spring of 1863, the Army of Virginia totaled approximately seventy-five thousand men with two hundred seventy-five pieces of artillery of varying caliber.

Three Confederate prisoners of war pose along a rail fence in Gettysburg. Seasoned veterans such as these men became increasingly hard to replace during the final years of the war.

Seeking information on Lee's army, ten thousand Union cavalry under the command of General Alfred Pleasanton struck an equal number of Stuart's horsemen on June 9th. The resulting battle of Brandy Station, Va., the largest cavalry battle of the war, was a tactical draw, but it did demonstrate how much improved the North's cavalry arm had become. Pleasanton had surprised Stuart at Brandy Station, causing him great embarrassment.

The Army of Northern Virginia crossed the Potomac River at Williamsport in mid June. Lee himself crossed the river on June 25. The situation had changed little since his last invasion in 1862 except that the odds were now further stacked against him. The South was running out of manpower while in the North, waves of immigrants were being pressed into service. Northern industry was pouring out weapons of war while in the South, many men went into battle unarmed. Although it would be going too far to say Lee had a fatalistic "conquer or die" attitude, this was Lee's last chance to win the war.

By July 1, his advance units had pushed as far as Carlisle and York in southern Pennsylvania. On that day, at the town of Gettysburg, a minor skirmish broke out between some Confederate infantrymen and some dismounted Union cavalry. Lee had not wished to provoke a general engagement at this time but gave orders that his scattered command concentrate at this important crossroads when engagement began. Long before he reached Gettysburg, word arrived that Hooker was no longer commanding the Union army. On June 28, Lincoln sacked Hooker and replaced him with Major General George G. Meade. Lee remarked, "We will not move to Harrisburg, as we expected, but instead will go over to Gettysburg and see what General Meade is after. Meade will commit no blunder in my front, and if I make one he will make haste to take advantage of it."

By moving quickly, Lee was able to win a significant victory on July 1, but his troops failed to take the high ground southeast of Gettysburg. It was a missed opportunity that would have enormous consequences. As the Union army arrived on the field it settled in atop Culp's Hill, Cemetery Ridge, and Little Round Top. Pushing the Union army back to high ground, he formed a defense line in the shape of a fishhook. For the next two days, Lee assaulted the Union "fishhook," first on the flanks on July 2, and then, in the center of the line on July 3. Longstreet, whose men had repelled Burnside at Fredericksburg, knew the strength of such a position and